Paul Shipton

LEVEL 1

SCHOLASTIC

JEWISH COMMUNITY SECONDARY SCHOOL

Written by: Paul Shipton

Publisher: Jacquie Bloese

Editor: Clare Gray

Designer: Dawn Wilson

Picture research: Pupak Navabpour

Photo credits:

Cover: S Simon/Press Association Images.

Pages 4 & 5: Popperfoto, AFP/Getty Images; AP/Press Association Images; B Costa, C Ferrari/ Reuters; E Peterson/ Eyevine.

Page 6: Hulton/Getty Images.

Pages 9 & 10: AM29/iStockphoto; Popperfoto/Getty Images.

Pages 12 & 13: Popperfoto/Getty Images; Y Arthus-Betrand/ Corbis.

Pages 14 & 15: S Mitchell/Press Association Images; L'Equipe/Offside.

Pages 17, 19 & 21: Popperfoto/Getty Images; Bettmann/ Corbis; AP/Press Association Images.

Pages 22, 23 & 25: Popperfoto/Getty Images; AP/ Press Association Images.

Pages 26 & 27: Keystone/Eyevine; J Cooke/Sports Illustrated/Getty Images.

Pages 28, 29 & 30: British Film Institute; J Ngwenya/ Reuters; S Simon/Press Association Images.

Pages 32 & 33: G Black/iStockphoto; M Brandt, F Monteforte/AFP/Getty Images.

Pages 34 & 35: B Thomas, P Ugarte/AFP/Getty Images.

Pages 36 & 37: D Turnley/Getty Images; Rex Features.

Mary Glasgow Magazines (Scholastic Ltd.)
Euston House
24 Eversholt Street
London NW1 IDB

Printed in Singapore

Contents

Page

PELÉ

As a teenager, Pelé was already a special footballer.

Pelé's father Dondinho played football, but he had many problems with injuries.

Celeste, Pelé's mother, did not want him to be a footballer.

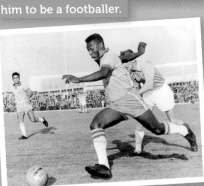

Rosemeri was Pelé's wife from 1965.

Pelé in Sweden, 1960

Pelé with his family

Pelé and his second wife, Assíria

Children's hospital in Curitiba, in the south of Brazil

PLACES

Bauru: Pelé's family moved to this town in Brazil when he was four years old.

Santos: Pelé's first big football club was in this city. It is close to Brazil's biggest city, São Paulo.

Sweden: Pelé played at his first World Cup here.

Mexico: He played his last World Cup in Mexico.

New York: In 1975, Pelé started to play for a football team in New York in the United States.

GOAL 1000!

On November 19th, 1969, there was a football game between two Brazilian football clubs – Santos and Vasco da Gama. The weather was terrible, but thousands of fans were there. They wanted to watch this important game for Santos' star player, Pelé. At twenty-nine years old, he was already the most famous footballer in the world.

In the second half, one of the Vasco players fouled a Santos player. Pelé's team had a penalty! Someone gave the ball to Pelé. He put it down and looked at the other team's goalkeeper.

Then Pelé took the penalty. The goalkeeper went to the left and the ball went to the right. GOAL! But this goal was special: it was Pelé's 1000th! The fans shouted and danced in the rain. Some ran on the pitch. Someone gave Pelé a new shirt to wear. It had a new number on it – 1000! It was a fantastic night for Pelé and for football. It was not a big surprise for fans of the sport. To them, Pelé was the best player in the world.

But twenty years before this night, life was very different for Pelé … .

CHAPTER 1
Life before 'Pelé'

At first, Pelé's name wasn't 'Pelé'! It was Edson Arantes do Nascimento, but his family called him 'Dico'. They lived in a small town, Três Corações in Brazil. In 1944, Dico's father, Dondinho, took a new job in the town of Bauru. Dico was four when the family moved there.

Dondinho worked and played for Bauru's football club, but he had a lot of problems with injuries. The family didn't have a lot of money. Seven of them – Dico, his mother, father, brother, sister, grandmother and uncle – lived in one small house. Dico started to do jobs to help his family. When he was eight, he cleaned shoes at the town's train station.

But after school and work, there was always football. Children in Brazil *loved* football, and this was true for Dico. He and his young brother Zoca played in the streets with the other children. They didn't wear any shoes and they didn't have a good football. Sometimes they used old clothes to make a ball!

'What do you want to do with your life?' his father asked one day.

Dico loved football, but he had other ideas. 'I love aeroplanes,' he answered. 'I want to work with them.'

And so he went to school and worked for this dream. But then one day an aeroplane came down in Bauru and someone died. When Dico heard this, his dream of a job with aeroplanes ended.

He still played football every evening and every weekend. He learned a lot about the sport from his father. Every year he was better and better.

Dondinho saw this. 'He's fast and strong. He can run

with the ball and kick well with both feet,' he told Dico's mother, Celeste.

Celeste didn't care. She wanted a good job for her son – not football! But it was too late. Football was Dico's life now. Around this time, Dico's friends started to call him a new name – 'Pelé'. Where did this come from? When he lived in Três Corações, Dico liked to watch his father's team. The other players called the goalkeeper 'Bilé'. Little Dico wanted to be a goalkeeper 'like Bilé'! Years after this, his friends in Bauru heard this name as 'Pelé'. At first, Dico did *not* like his new name!

BRAZIL

Brazil is the biggest country in South America – 8,550,000 km². The Amazon River – the biggest river (and the second longest) in the world – runs through the north of the country. The Amazon rainforest is home to more different living things than anywhere in the world.

Facts

Capital: Brasilia

Biggest city: São Paulo

Number of people: around 192,000,000 (in 2010)

Language: Most Brazilians speak Portuguese, but there are more than 200 languages in Brazil!

Amazon rainforest

Most Brazilians live in cities – twenty cities there have more than 1,000,000 people. São Paulo and Rio de Janeiro are two of the biggest cities in the world. Brazil is not a poor country, but many of its people are poor.

Around 2,000,000 native people lived in the country before the Portuguese arrived in 1500. The Portuguese took many slaves from Africa to Brazil. Some of Pelé's family were slaves in the 1800s.

From around the 1850s, more people from Italy, Germany and other parts of Europe moved to Brazil; in the early 1900s, large groups of Japanese people moved there. Today Brazil is a mix of these different people.

> **What do these words mean?**
> **You can use a dictionary.**
> capital   north   rainforest   native
> people   slave   mix

CHAPTER 2
The team with no shoes

In 1951, Pelé and some friends started their own team. They were poor and they still played without shoes. Some people called them 'the team with no shoes'.

Soon a man from the city gave them money. Now the team had shoes and a new name – *Amériquinho*. They played in a tournament for all of the city's young teams. They won, and Pelé was the team's star player.

Two years later, Bauru Athletic Club (BAC) asked Pelé to join their boys' team. Pelé was very happy. BAC was his father's old team. 'It was one of the most exciting days of my life,' Pelé said later.

Pelé (second from the left) with his family

Pelé was thirteen now, and he started to learn more and more about football. The manager of BAC's boys' team, Waldemar de Brito, was a famous man in Brazilian football. When he was young, he played for Brazil. He was a good manager and teacher, and Pelé learned a lot from him.

To de Brito, Pelé was special. When he was fifteen, a big team from Rio de Janeiro wanted the young player. His mother wasn't happy. 'My Dico is only fifteen!' she cried. 'He's not going to Rio!'

But nothing stopped Pelé's love for the sport. De Brito knew this and called a football club in the smaller city of Santos, not far from São Paulo. After a few phone calls, the club asked Pelé to play for them.

It was like a dream for the young footballer. He and his father left on an early train for São Paulo. His mother and brother cried at the station when the train left.

'I want to make some money and buy a house for my mum,' Pelé told Dondinho.

His father smiled. 'Don't dream yet,' he said.

CHAPTER 3
Pelé arrives!

De Brito met Pelé and Dondinho at the station and the three took a bus to Santos. Pelé looked out of the window and saw the Atlantic Ocean for the first time. He said goodbye to his father and his new life started.

Pelé lived with other players in one of the club's buildings. It was exciting to be there, but he was far from his home and family. More than once he tried to go home. On one of these times, his new friends on the team took him and his bags back from the train station. Years after, Pelé called these new friends his 'football family'.

He practised every day and learned a lot. He played for one of Santos' young teams. Soon the manager asked him to play for the club's first team. Still only fifteen and not very big, Pelé walked out in Santos' white-and-black shirt as part of the team. The Santos fans did not know much about this new player. That changed when Pelé scored! Many years later, Pelé met the other team's goalkeeper. For all those years, the goalkeeper told everybody: 'The great Pelé scored his first Santos goal against *me*!'

Pelé (right) with some of the Santos team

Pelé was the youngest player for any Brazilian team, but more and more goals followed. He scored thirty-two for Santos in his first year. Pelé practised his game every day. He kicked better with his right foot, and so he practised with his left. He wanted his left foot to be strong too. He also practised heading the ball. Soon he was bigger and stronger.

Maracanã Stadium

In the summer of the next year, 1957, the club played in a tournament at the famous Maracanã Stadium in Rio de Janeiro. Pelé was the tournament's top scorer – six goals in four games! At just sixteen, he was the favourite of the Santos fans.

Brazilians started to ask, 'Maybe Pelé can play for the Brazilian team?' He played his first game for Brazil in 1957, against Argentina. Brazil didn't win, but Pelé scored their only goal.

CHAPTER 4
On top of the world

The year of 1958 was a special year for football fans. It was the World Cup, and this year the tournament was in Sweden. Brazil's managers named their team at the end of 1957. At the time, Pelé was in Bauru to see his family. He sat by the radio and listened as the managers read the names. Suddenly he heard his own name! At just seventeen years old, he was in Brazil's team for the biggest football tournament in the world!

The tournament started in July. For the first time in his life, Pelé was on an aeroplane to a different country! The team was happy and ready for the tournament, and Pelé

The World Cup

The World Cup is the world's biggest football tournament. The finals are every four years. For the three years before this, lots of teams around the world play to decide the teams in the finals. Until 1982, 16 teams played in the finals; from 1982 until 1998, 24 teams played. Now 32 teams play in the finals.

In the finals, the teams start in groups. A team has to play all the other teams in its group. After this, the best teams meet in a knock-out tournament.

What does this word mean?
You can use a dictionary.
knock-out

loved Sweden. He liked Gothenburg's* dance clubs and listening to music. The Swedish girls loved the Brazilian players too!

Pelé with some Swedish fans in 1958

Pelé had a leg injury and so he did not play in Brazil's first two games. But he was ready for the third game.

 Brazil v Soviet Union†
Brazil won 2–0. Pelé helped his team to score the second goal with a beautiful pass. For many football fans around the world, this game was their first look at the young star from Brazil.

Brazil v Wales
Wales was also a strong team, with a very good goalkeeper. There were no goals for a long time. Then, in the second half, the great Brazilian player Didi

* Gothenberg is a big town in Sweden
† Soviet Union: From 1922 until 1991, Russia and other countries in East Europe made one big country, the Soviet Union, or USSR.

passed a high ball to Pelé. The young player kicked it up and over the head of a Welsh player and ran around him. Then he kicked the ball and scored. It was a fantastic goal. It was Pelé's first goal in a World Cup.

Brazil v France

Brazil played their fast, exciting game against France. Pelé was fantastic. The teenager scored a goal in the second half. Then he scored again – and again. In the end, Brazil won 5–2. It was a great win, and a fantastic game for Pelé – three goals in a World Cup game! Now everybody in the world knew about this special young footballer. His way of playing the game was beautiful to watch.

Brazil v Sweden

Now Brazil was in the final against the home team. Most of the fans at the game were Swedish. They were happy when their team scored in the fourth minute of the game. But soon the Swedish fans weren't happy. Brazil played fantastically. They scored two times in the first half. Pelé scored the first goal of the second half. After another goal for both teams, Pelé scored the game's last goal with his head. It was a beautiful goal – even the Swedish goalkeeper said this! Brazil won 5–2 and Pelé was the star of the game.

Brazilian fans there danced and shouted. It was all too much for Pelé: he started to cry. He was still only a teenager, but now he was one of the most famous players in the world.

CHAPTER 5
The girl at the game

Back in Brazil, life changed for Pelé's family. Suddenly, lots of people wanted to meet them. This new life was a big surprise for Dondinho and Celeste; they needed new clothes for all the parties now!

On the pitch for Santos, Pelé was still fantastic. In 1959, he scored 127 goals for the team. Off the pitch, his life was busy and interesting. After football, he had a lot of fun with his good friends from the team. They went to a basketball game one Saturday night. The others watched the game, but not Pelé. He saw a pretty girl at the game and he just watched her! Her name was Rosemeri Cholbi.

Rosemeri worked in a music shop and Pelé went there to see her.

'I don't like football,' Rosemeri said to him. Pelé didn't care. He wanted to be her boyfriend.

But Rosemeri was young. She was only fourteen. Pelé

Pelé went into the Brazilian army in 1959

was three years older than her. She asked him to come to her home that weekend. Rosemeri's father was a Santos fan, and Pelé enjoyed his time with the family. He started to go and see Rosemeri and her family often. Sometimes he and Rosemeri went to the cinema, but someone from her family always came with them.

Before the end of 1959, Pelé was eighteen. At that time in Brazil, all young men went into the army for a year.

At first he didn't want to go. 'I helped my country at the World Cup. Do I need to do it again in the army?' he asked. The answer was 'Yes!' But army life was not so different for Pelé. He still played for Santos and Brazil, but now he played for the army's football team, too!

Santos was soon the top team in Brazil. In 1961 and 1962, they won the Brazil Cup*. In 1962, they also won the *Copa Libertadores*† and the Club World Cup‡. They played in other countries, too. Everybody wanted to see Pelé.

Soon it was time for the next World Cup, and Brazil had high hopes for the 1962 tournament in Chile. But just before the World Cup, Pelé had a bad injury. Was he OK to play?

In fact, he played in the first game – against Mexico – and he scored one of Brazil's two goals. But in the next game his injury was back. It was Pelé's last game of the tournament. In the final Brazil played Czechoslovakia and won 3–1. Pelé was happy for his team and country, but part of him was sad. He didn't want just to watch. He wanted to *play*.

Back in Brazil, he was soon on the pitch for Santos again, and the team was still on top. They won the *Copa Libertadores* in 1963, the Brazil Cup in 1963, 1964 and 1965, and the Club World Cup again in 1963. The Santos fans had a new name for Pelé, *O Rei* – 'the King'! In one game in 1964 'the King' scored *eight* goals!

---

* The Brazil Cup (*Taça Brasil*) was a tournament for the best teams in Brazil.
† The *Copa Libertadores* was a tournament for football clubs in all of South America.
‡ The Club World Cup was a tournament for the best club teams from around the world.

In 1965, Rosemeri was old enough to marry. Pelé went out in a little boat with her father. They often fished together, but today Pelé had an important question.

'I want to marry Rosemeri,' said Pelé.

The older man didn't answer. He wanted to talk about this with his wife. Pelé sat in the boat for hours as Rosemeri's father fished. It was one of the most difficult times of Pelé's life! At last they went back to the house and Rosemeri's family gave their answer. It was 'Yes'!

Pelé and Rosemeri married early in 1966 and went to Europe on holiday together. Later that year Pelé was back in Europe again. It was the World Cup and this time it was in England.

Pelé and Rosemeri on holiday in Rome in 1966

CHAPTER 6
The worst World Cup

Pelé doesn't remember the 1966 World Cup in England happily. Brazil usually went to the tournament with twenty-two players. In 1966 they took forty-three players. To Pelé, the team wasn't strong. They never knew the players before any game. Pelé and some others weren't happy before the start of the tournament.

Brazil's games were in Liverpool, a big English city, and the team stayed near here. Pelé did not know much English at this time. When English people talked to him, he always answered with the same words: 'Yes, yes, yes, I know, thank you!'

But Pelé had a bigger problem. The world knew all about Pelé now, and some players on other teams had a plan: 'We can't play better than Pelé, but we can foul him!'

Brazil v Bulgaria

Brazil won their first game, against Bulgaria, and Pelé scored one of his team's two goals. But the Bulgarian players fouled and kicked at him through the game.

Brazil v Hungary

The managers decided *not* to play Pelé in Brazil's next game. And so the team met Hungary *without* the best player in the world. It was a bad idea: Hungary won 3–1!

Brazil v Portugal

The Brazilian managers changed the team again for the next game, against Portugal. Pelé was back, and one of the world's other great players, Eusebio, played for Portugal. This was exciting for football fans: 'Who is better? Pelé or Eusebio?' But the game gave no answers. It was worse for Pelé than the Bulgaria game – Portuguese players fouled Pelé again and again. And no one stopped them! After a last, terrible foul, Pelé was out of the game with an injury. In the end, Portugal won 3–1. It was difficult to believe it: Brazil's World Cup games were over!

It was a terrible day for Brazilian football. The team and all the fans back home were sad and angry about the tournament. That year the home team, England, won the World Cup. But on the day of the final, Pelé was already home.

After the 'worst World Cup', Pelé's love of football died a little. Santos was still the number one team in Brazil. But the team played game after game, and Pelé was tired with this life. Everything changed in January, 1967, when he and Rosemeri had their first child. They named their little daughter Kelly Cristina. Suddenly Pelé saw the world with new eyes. With his new daughter, Pelé started to love his life – and football – again.

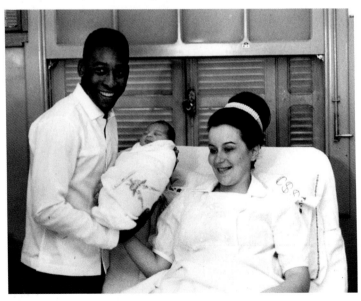

CHAPTER 7
'The beautiful team'

Pelé remembers 1968 as the most important year for
Santos. They were in five big tournaments and they won
all five. From this time comes one of sport's most famous
photos. In it, you can see Pelé do his 'bicycle kick' over
his head.

Pelé was still the club's star, and Santos gave him more
money than the other players. Money came from other
places too. Pelé was the most famous face in Brazil; now
he used his famous smile to sell things on TV. On the
pitch, Pelé still scored in game after game, and in 1969 he
scored that famous 1000th goal.

That year Brazilians started to think about the next
World Cup, but Pelé had a surprise for the fans: 'I'm not
playing for Brazil again.' He was a father now and, at

twenty-nine, he was older than the other players. But 1966 was a very bad end to his life in world football. Pelé wanted to finish on top! He thought again about the World Cup. Slowly his ideas changed and he decided to join the team again.

The 1970 World Cup in Mexico was different from other World Cups. For the first time, fans around the world watched the games in colour on live television. Now more than one billion people saw Pelé's fantastic football!

Brazil v Czechoslovakia*

This was Brazil's first game. The score was 1–1 when Pelé had the ball. He was almost in the Brazilian half but he kicked the ball long and high, about 50 metres! The ball went over the goalkeeper's head. It was *almost* a goal, and it was one of the most fantastic kicks in any World Cup! Brazil won 4–1. They were on their way!

Brazil v England

The 1966 winners, England, were very strong at the back. For once, Brazil didn't play with lots of fast, exciting passes from player to player. They used more long, high passes from the back to the players at the front. At the time, this was the 'English game'. This was a good plan, and Brazil scored the game's only goal.

Fans around the world asked: 'Can any team stop Brazil now?' The answer was 'No!' Brazil won against Romania, Peru and Uruguay. Now they were in the World Cup final!

---

* Czechoslovakia was a European country from 1918 until 1992. Now the old Czechoslovakia is two countries, The Czech Republic and Slovakia.

Brazil v Italy

The final game was in Mexico City's Aztec Stadium on June 21, 1970. Pelé scored the first goal with his head. Italy scored next, but after that the game was Brazil's. They played fantastically. It was beautiful to watch. Many people think the Brazilian team of the 1970 World Cup was the best football team of all time. People called them 'the beautiful team', and they called their football 'the beautiful game'. In the end, Brazil won 4–1. For fans around the world, football was the winner that day.

Brazil and Pelé – World Cup winners

Pelé was the first man to be in three winning World Cup teams – 1958, 1962 and 1970. Later, he called the 1970 final 'one of my best games in a Brazil shirt'. It was a good game for his last World Cup.

CHAPTER 8
Goodbye to Santos

Pelé left Mexico before the other Brazilian players because he wanted to see Rosemeri. In August she had their second child – a boy, Edinho.

With two children now, Pelé started to think about the important things in life. 'What am I?' he asked. 'Just a footballer?' When he was little, he didn't do very well in school. Pelé wanted to change this now; he wanted to go 'back to school'. He gave a lot of time to his school work. After two years of this, he went to Santos University for three more years.

Pelé still played for Santos during this time. But he decided to stop playing for Brazil now. He played his last Brazil game on July 18, 1971, against Yugoslavia. After the game, thousands of fans shouted, 'Stay! Stay!'

Three years later, on October 2, 1974, Pelé played his last Santos game. After just twenty minutes, Pelé took the ball in his hands and ran to the centre of the pitch. He put the ball down and looked around at all the fans. Pelé cried

Pelé says goodbye

as they shouted for him. He took off his Santos shirt for the last time and said goodbye.

But just months after this, an American team, New York Cosmos, asked Pelé to play for them. The money was good – around $4,500,000. But Pelé also wanted to teach Americans more about the sport.

Pelé playing for New York Cosmos

The family moved to New York. Life was very different here. It was an exciting time in the city and Pelé met lots of famous film stars and singers at clubs and restaurants.

American newspapers wrote a lot about Pelé, and the Cosmos games were always full. Pelé still played fantastic football but he was slower now. After almost two years with Cosmos, it was time to say goodbye to football.

On October 1, 1977, when Pelé was almost thirty-seven, he played his last game. It was against his old Brazilian club Santos. Thousands of fans were there, and the game was on television in thirty-eight countries. Pelé played the first half for Cosmos and he scored a good goal. He played the next half in his Santos shirt one last time.

With the goal in that last game, Pelé finished his fantastic life in football – 1,281 goals in 1,363 games.

CHAPTER 9
Life after football

Life after football was still very busy for Pelé. He wasn't a player now, but football was still very important in his life. He worked to help the sport in Brazil and around the world. He was often on TV to talk about important games. He still lived in New York, but he went all over the world for work. He did a lot of charity work; most of all, he wanted to help children in poor countries.

In 1978, Rosemeri had their third child, Jennifer, but this was not a happy time for the family. Pelé was away from home a lot, and Rosemeri did not like this. Just a week after Jennifer arrived, Rosemeri left Pelé and their time together ended.

In 1981, Pelé did something very different: he was in a Hollywood film, *Escape to Victory*, with Sylvester Stallone! The film was about football and other footballers were in it too. In one part of the film, Pelé scores a goal with his famous bicycle kick!

From left to right: Sylvester Stallone, Pelé, Michael Caine and film-maker, John Huston, working on *Escape to Victory*

Through his work for charity, Pelé met the most important people in the world: Ronald Reagan, Bill Clinton, even Nelson Mandela!

In 1994, Pelé married his second wife, Assíria. Three years later they had two children, Joshua and Celeste.

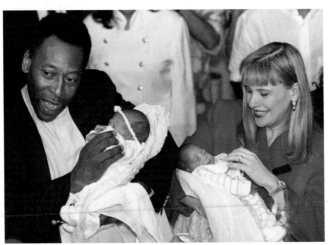

The family has homes in the United States, but now they spend more of their time in Brazil.

Today Pelé still loves football. His charity work still helps many children around the world too.

• • •

Over the years, Pelé scored with both feet and with his head. He passed the ball fantastically; he was fast and strong. But more than this, he could 'read' the game faster than anyone. Pelé called it a 'feel' for the game … And nobody had a better feel for the game than *O Rei*!

THE WORLD CUP

The World Cup is the greatest tournament in football. It started in 1930. Now, years later, it is the biggest tournament in sport.

In 2006, three billion people around the world watched the final between France and Italy. With each tournament more and more people watch the World Cup. It is very expensive for the host country to have the World Cup there. But the tournament brings lots of money and new jobs. In South Africa in 2010, there were over 400,000 new jobs because of the World Cup.

FIVE WORLD CUP STORIES

YEAR: 1930
HOST COUNTRY: Uruguay
Only thirteen teams played in the tournament because some European teams didn't want to go all the way to South America to play!
WINNERS: Uruguay

YEAR: 1950
HOST COUNTRY: Brazil
This was the only cup with no knockout tournament and so no final. When Uruguay won, Pelé's father Dondinho (and many other Brazilians) cried.
WINNERS: Uruguay

YEAR: 1966

HOST COUNTRY: England

Before the tournament, somebody took the trophy! The police looked everywhere. A dog found the trophy under a bush!

WINNERS: England

YEAR: 2006

HOST COUNTRY: Germany

It was a sad end to the World Cup for France's great Zinedine Zidane. In the final, he fouled an Italian player with his head, and the referee sent off Zidane. At last, Italy won on penalties.

WINNERS: Italy

YEAR: 1986

HOST COUNTRY: Mexico

In a quarter-final game with England, Argentina's Diego Maradona famously scored a goal with his hand.

WINNERS: Argentina

The biggest winners! And the country with the most World Cup winning teams? Brazil, of course! They won in 1958, 1962, 1970, 1994 and 2002. No other country was in every World Cup tournament. And in 2014, Brazil is the host for the second time!

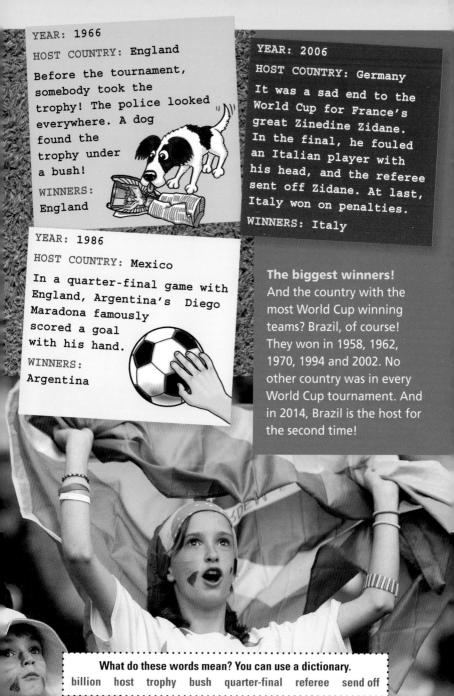

What do these words mean? You can use a dictionary.
billion   host   trophy   bush   quarter-final   referee   send off

FIVE OF THE BEST

Who was the best football player ever? Football fans will give you lots of different answers. It is difficult to compare players from different times and different positions on the pitch. Here are five of football's great players:

Franz Beckenbauer

Country: West Germany

Position: defender

Born: 11 September, 1945

Beckenbauer was a defender, but he also scored goals for his country. In 1974, he was the captain of West Germany's World Cup-winning team. Then in 1990, he was the manager of his country's World Cup-winning team.

Johan Cruyff

Country: Holland

Position: striker

Born: 25 April, 1947

Holland's most important player in the 1970s, Cruyff was difficult to play against: he changed positions with other players and ran all over the pitch.

What do these words mean? You can use a dictionary.

position   defender   captain   striker   midfielder   referee

Diego Maradona

Country: Argentina

Position: midfielder

Born: 30 October, 1960

Maradona was fantastic at taking the ball past players and scoring. Fans called his second goal against England in the 1986 quarter-final the 'Goal of the Century'.

Zinedine Zidane

Country: France

Position: midfielder

Born: 23 June, 1972

Like many people from Algeria, Zidane's family moved to France in the 1950s. But Zidane never played for Algeria. He played for France in three World Cups. In the 1998 World Cup final he scored two goals against Brazil. His team won 3-0. The referee sent Zidane off in the 2006 final, but he was still the 'Player of the Tournament'.

Ronaldo

Country: Brazil

Position: striker

Born: 22 September, 1976

Some fans think that Ronaldo is football's greatest striker ever. With 15 goals, he is the top scorer in the World Cup finals ever – more than the great Pelé!

Of course, all football fans have their favourites – France's Michel Platini, Portugal's Cristiano Ronaldo, England's David Beckham, and many more. And, of course, there's 'the King' ... Pelé!

Celebrity and

Pelé gives a lot of time and money to many charities around the world. Other celebrities do work for charity too. They give their money, but they also help to tell people about important world problems.

David Beckham

Beckham is the most famous English footballer of our time. He does a lot of work for many charities. In 2007, he went to the African country of Sierra Leone with the organization. In this poor country, one in four children die of illnesses before they are five. Beckham wants more people to know about this terrible problem. He hopes his work can help.

Beckham meets some young footballers in Sierra Leone

charity

Help from Hollywood

Film stars Angelina Jolie and her husband Brad Pitt work for many charities, too. In 2006 they gave more than eight million dollars to charity. Jolie does a lot of work in different countries for the UNHCR. The UNHCR works to help refugees around the world.

Charity work is also very important to film star George Clooney. He gives millions of dollars to charities every year. After the terrible earthquake in Haiti in 2010, he planned a television show. Millions of people watched the show and gave money for the people of Haiti.

Bono

In the world of music, singer Bono from the Irish band U2, is very busy with charity work. He works with ONE. ONE helps people in the world's poorest places. He speaks to the most important people in the world about this work.

> **What do these words mean? You can use a dictionary.**
> celebrity   illness   refugee   dollar   earthquake   show

GOAL 1000–CHAPTER 3

Before you read

You can use your dictionary.

1 Match these words with the sentences.

aeroplane fan goal goalkeeper kick manager pitch

a) This person chooses the players in a football team.

b) You can fly in this.

c) This is between 90m and 120m long.

d) A good one goes to all of his team's games.

e) Only this person can use his or her hands on the ball.

f) You do this with your leg.

g) A good footballer can get lots of these.

2 Complete the sentences.

foul half penalty practise score tournament win

a) He is good on the guitar because he ... every day.

b) There were sixteen teams in the ... .

c) Never ... other players in a football game.

d) One ... of a football game is 45 minutes.

e) She had a fantastic game: she ... three goals!

f) One of their players used his hands. It's a ... !

g) They're a great team – we never ... against them!

3 What do you already know about Pelé? Try these questions.

a) Where is he from?

b) Was he a rich or poor child?

c) Did he always want to be a footballer?

d) What was his first big team?

Now read and find the answers.

After you read

4 Are these sentences Right (✓) or Wrong (✗).

a) Pelé played for Santos.

b) As a child, he always wanted to be a footballer.

c) His mother did not want Pelé to be a footballer.

d) Waldemar de Brito played on Pelé's first team in Bauru.

e) Pelé went to play for a club in Rio.

5 Choose the right answer.

  a) Where did Pelé live at first at Santos?

    i) in a hotel

    ii) in one of the club's buildings

  b) In the early days at Santos, how did Pelé feel?

    i) At times he wanted to go home and be with his family.

    ii) He never thought about his friends or family.

  c) What happened in his first game for the Santos first team?

    i) He scored a goal.

    ii) He took a penalty.

  d) What happened in the tournament in 1957?

    i) Santos won six games.

    ii) Pelé scored more goals than any other player.

CHAPTERS 4-6

Before you read

You can use your dictionary for these questions.

6 Complete the sentences with these words.

  army   final   injury   king   marry   pass

  a) He didn't play because he had a bad ... .

  b) 'Quick! ... the ball to me!'

  c) Kate and John are going to ... in the summer.

  d) In some countries, all young people go into the ... for a year.

  e) The two best teams met in the ... .

  f) Some countries have still got a ... .

7 Read the titles of chapters 4, 5 and 6. What do you think?

  a) In which chapter does Pelé marry?

  b) In which chapter does Brazil win the biggest tournament in world football?

  c) In which chapter does a different team win the biggest tournament in world football?

After you read

8 Answer the questions.

   a) Why didn't Pelé play in the first two games of the 1958 World Cup?

   b) Who did Brazil play in the 1958 final?

   c) What did Pelé do after the game?

   d) Where did he first see Rosemeri?

   e) Why was Pelé sad at the 1962 World Cup?

9 Correct the sentences.

   a) The 1966 World Cup was in Bulgaria.

   b) Pelé did not want to play in the game against Hungary.

   c) Eusebio was a famous player for Brazil.

   d) Pelé left the Portugal game because he fouled a player.

   e) During the 1966 World Cup final, Pelé was in the stadium.

CHAPTERS 7-9

Before you read

10 Do you give money to a **charity**? Do you help any charities in other ways? Why / why not?

After you read

11 Put these sentences in the correct order.

   a) Pele went 'back to school'.

   b) He went to a team in New York.

   c) He scored his famous 1000th goal.

   d) He played his last game in Brazil for Santos.

   e) Brazil won their third World Cup.

12 What do you think?

   a) Why do many football fans still remember Pelé as the best player?

   b) In what way was he 'more than a footballer'?